Gallery Books
Editor: Peter Fallon

VERA OF LAS VEGAS

Paul Muldoon

VERA OF
LAS VEGAS

Gallery Books

PR
6063
.U367
V4
2001

Vera of Las Vegas
is first published
simultaneously in paperback
and in a clothbound edition
on 31 May 2001.

The Gallery Press
Loughcrew
Oldcastle
County Meath
Ireland

ISBN 1 85235 283 3 (*paperback*)
      1 85235 284 1 (*clothbound*)

The Gallery Press acknowledges the financial assistance of An Chomhairle Ealaíon / The Arts Council, Ireland, and the Arts Council of Northern Ireland.

47149594

Dramatis Personae

TACO, a forty-five year old man, originally from Northern Ireland. He's now an illegal resident of the Bronx, New York, where he drives a cab.

DUMDUM, his lifelong friend, also forty-five and living illegally in the Bronx where he tends bar.

DOLL, a forty year old woman, formerly a blackjack dealer, now an undercover agent for the Immigration and Naturalization Service.

VERA, a lapdancer from Las Vegas.

TRENCH, a shady character.

TRILBY, a shady character.

CHORUS, Flight attendants, Romans, Pequods, casino girls, strippers, lapdancers, a wedding chapel choir.

Vera of Las Vegas was first performed, in workshop, by the University of Nevada (Las Vegas) Opera Theatre in March 1996.

'It was not Café Society. It was Nescafé Society.'
— Noël Coward

Prologue

We find TACO *in what must be an interrogation centre, somewhere in Northern Ireland. He is slumped back on a chair, hands cuffed. Directly above him is an intensely bright lamp that swings violently as* TRENCH *and* TRILBY *take turns to slap his face, as if to bring him round. We hear the judder of his own blood in* TACO's *ears as the slapping continues. This judder crossfades into the shudder of a plane landing as* TACO *slips into unconsciousness. The lamp suddenly flies up and* TACO, TRILBY *and* TRENCH *are plunged into darkness. The shudder of the plane crossfades to the susurrus of a chorus.*

I

CHORUS   Ante up. Double down. Hit me. Fold. No more bets. Snake eyes. Stick.

    The susurrus builds to a frenzy of shouts as the lights come up on the luggage claim area at Las Vegas airport. The distant shudder of planes taking off and landing continues. A CHORUS *of flight attendants dressed in powder blue swank by and congregate near a bank of courtesy phones. Opposite the phones is a bank of slot machines, being played by toga-clad Romans.* TACO *shuffles on, clearly disaffected, followed by* DUMDUM, *who's pushing a trolley piled with carry-on luggage.* DUMDUM *wears a cheap suit,* TACO *jeans and a leather jacket. Both are a little tipsy.*

TACO   I should have known better than to let you book the flights.

    He points to his ticket.

    LAX, it says here. Yes? No?

DUMDUM I said I was sorry, Taco.
TACO   Lax, Dumdum.
DUMDUM   I'm very . . .
TACO Very lax.
DUMDUM   No one said we'd have to change
     planes a couple of times.
TACO   Extremely loose.
     Now we're stuck here for — what? A day? Two
     days?
DUMDUM Two *hours*.
TACO Two days stuck on a landing strip
     in the middle of nowhere.

> DOLL *enters in the company of an exceptionally*
> *attractive colleague, who joins the other flight*
> *attendants.* DOLL, *facing away from us, picks up a*
> *telephone.*

DUMDUM   The centre
     of the universe, Taco.
TACO   The centre-*fold.*
DUMDUM We're at the heart of something here.
TACO   The heart?
DUMDUM The heart of America.

> *A delegation of Pequods dressed in extremely sharp*
> *suits but wearing quivers and carrying bows*
> *enters.* TACO *conjures an hourglass figure as he*
> *continues to ogle* DOLL's *colleague.*

TACO   Built of sand.
     Don't you just love a woman in a suit?

> DUMDUM *is getting in on the act.*

DUMDUM Those little girls blue . . .
TACO   In their uni*forms.*

> TACO *and* DUMDUM *are greatly taken with their*

own wit and repartee. A distorted female voice comes over the intercom.

INTERCOM Attention, please . . . Would the Pequod delega-
tion . . .

The Pequods turn as one towards the intercom as the message breaks up.

DUMDUM Not that we can call them 'girls' any more.
We know only too well that just won't . . .

TACO   Fly?

DUMDUM Same with 'one-armed bandits'.

TACO makes a lewd gesture as he calls out to the attractive flight attendant.

TACO   'Little girl blue . . .

DUMDUM 'Physically challenged . . .

TACO   Come blow my horn.'

DUMDUM Freedom fighters.'

TACO and DUMDUM are now overwhelmed by them-selves.

INTERCOM Attention, please . . . Would Mist . . .

TACO 'Squeeze my lemon . . . '

DUMDUM   'Baby, squeeze my lemon,
till the juice . . .

TACO plays a riff on air guitar.

TACO   till the juice runs down my leg.'

TACO and DUMDUM are doubled up with laughter.

INTERCOM Would Mr Taco Bell
please pick up the nearest courtesy phone.

TACO *and* DUMDUM *freeze. They're completely stunned.* DOLL *turns to face us, phone in hand. Five beats.* TACO *makes to move.*

DUMDUM No, Taco . . .
Taco Was that 'Bell' she said or 'Tell'?

TACO *again makes to move in the direction of the phones.*

DUMDUM No, Taco . . .
TACO   It's somebody taking a hand
out of us, that's all.
DUMDUM   Who, though? They all think
we're still back in the Big fucking Apple.
TACO Not at the cab company . . . Not at the bar.
They know . . .
DUMDUM   But they don't know we're on our way
to take part in *Wheel of Fortune* . . . Unless . . .
TACO I swear . . .

TACO *again makes to move for the phone.*

DUMDUM   No . . . It's not on the level.

II

The CHORUS *of flight attendants gather round to listen to* DOLL, *who puts her hand over the mouthpiece of the phone.*

DOLL The pilot barely had time to level
out over La Guardia when all hell broke loose
in the shape of Taco Bell. 'Do you think
I might find,' says he, 'a place in your heart?'
Dumdum Devlin meanwhile had his hand on
my leg.

ATTENDANTS Why do men think that women who fly
are somehow flightier?
We were somewhere
over Minneapolis
when I consulted my little black book
and gave Vera a bell
from the galley.

ATTENDANTS Just because we spend our days
as galley-slaves in a blur of blue
doesn't mean we're whores.

DOLL I know her from the
Sands.
She used to work the bar
while I dealt blackjack at the casino.
So I arranged over the telephone
to meet her tonight in Delphine. A club just off
the Strip.
She'll help me stack the cards against these Irish
greenhorns
with their shiny faces and their shiny suits.

TACO *has picked up a courtesy phone.*

TACO Hello.
ATTENDANTS Just because we usually go out of our way
to be very, very, very
polite doesn't mean we won't tell

13

a couple of jerks like these . . .

TACO   Hello.

DOLL *uncovers the mouthpiece of the phone.*

DOLL   This is the
Visitor Centre . . .

ATTENDANTS Where to get off.

DOLL   Is that Mr Bell?

TACO   Maybe.

DOLL   We
missed
you by a whisker in New York.

TACO   Who are you?

DOLL

                                                    It's
bad form
to ask such questions, Mr Bell.

TACO   That so?

DOLL   We'd
more or less
decided, though things can always change,
to offer you a free night in Las Vegas. Hotel room.
Cash in hand.

TACO O Lord.

DOLL   You'll be met by one of our representa-
tives.

TACO   How manifold
are thy works, O Lord.

DOLL   Her name is Vera Loman.

TACO Vera?

DOLL   Vera. She'll be your personal escort. Girl
Friday. Gofer. Or more.

III

TACO covers the mouthpiece of the phone and turns to DUMDUM, who's been anxiously listening in.

DUMDUM Who is it, Taco? Is it them?

TACO No. It's not them.

DUMDUM It's
not more
of that INS shit?

TACO No.

DUMDUM INS. Imbeciles. Nincompoops.
Spineless
wonders.

TACO smiles as he sets down the receiver.

TACO No, Dumdum. It's a once-in-a-lifetime
chance.

DUMDUM Go suck a lemon.

TACO folds his hands across his chest.

TACO I'd like to suggest a slight change
in plan.

DUMDUM You know, the way you fold
your arms and hands,
you look just like your da.

TACO We can fly
to LA tomorrow.

DUMDUM Like your da and Jimmy
Lavelle
before Jimmy lost the leg.

TACO Why don't we hang loose
in Las Vegas, Dumdum, old heart,
for just one night?

DUMDUM Don't you ever stop to think
that there might be sand

in the ointment? A razor in the apple?
You know that if the boys in blue
ever catch up with us they'll throw the book
at us.

TACO   We're talking about one all-expenses-paid
day
in Las Vegas.

DOLL   Hello. Hello. Hello. Mr Bell?

TACO *lifts the receiver.*

TACO Yes. It's me.

DOLL   I don't know if I mentioned the suite,
Mr Bell, complete with mini-bar.

TACO   Iron?

DOLL   Yes.

TACO   Shoe-
horn?

DOLL Yes.

TACO   All mod cons. I can hardly say 'No'
to such a generous offer.

DOLL   Then take a limo to the
Strip.
We'll reimburse you. Meet Vera at six at the
dolphin.

TACO The dolphin?

DOLL   It's a statue near the Forum
Shops. Your driver will know the way.

TACO How will I know Vera?

DOLL   She'll be carrying *The
Economist.*

TACO *The Economist?*

DOLL   She'll know you.

TACO   She will? That's
very
intriguing.

DOLL   There are two statues. One of a centaur
and one of a dolphin. Meet Vera there.

TACO   And your

name?

DOLL   That I may not tell.

IV

DOLL *hangs up, as does* TACO, *who turns to* DUMDUM. TACO *and* DUMDUM *exit as if in a trance. The* CHORUS *of flight attendants, Romans, and Pequods gather round* DOLL.

ATTENDANTS Will they fall for it? How long before we can tell
if Taco and Dumdum are true to form
and fall for it?

ROMANS   They must think they'll saunter
back along the Appian Way
like two conquering heroes back from Gaul? Not
before Vera
comes galloping out of the Celtic mist
with her chariot and prancing four-in-hand?
Vera . . . Vera . . . Veracingetorix . . .

ATTENDANTS   They're just
two more
suckers who'll lose their billfolds
to Vera of Las Vegas. There'll be a lot less
of their flapdoodle when she turns them upside
down and shakes the change
out of their pockets. How long before these
flimflam men
might be persuaded not to think
that women who fly
are somehow flightier?

PEQUODS   For Vera embodies the
truth at the heart
of Vegas. Always presses the button for the lowest
level.
Always plays fast and loose.
Always breaks a leg.
Always somebody else's. She'll bury Dumdum
Devine and Taco Bell
up to their necks in sand.
She'll leave them staked out for a couple of days.
Then she'll cut off their balls. She'll cut out their

Adam's-apples.

> TRENCH *and* TRILBY, *two outrageously conspicuous plainclothesmen, enter and loom large in the background.*

ROMANS For Vera of Las Vegas wrote the book
on guerrilla warfare. Veracingetorix painting her
  body blue
with woad.

PEQUODS   She'll carry a belt of blue
beads and a bow . . .

ROMANS   She'll come galloping like
Godiva on the Godolphin
wearing a coney-skin suit.

> TRENCH *and* TRILBY *approach* DOLL *with all the surreptitiousness of which they're capable.* TRENCH *hands her a bulky manila envelope.* DOLL *exits in one direction,* TRENCH *and* TRILBY *in the other.*

PEQUODS She'll stake them out. She'll bind their wrists
  with strips
of wet rawhide. She'll shove a red-hot iron bar
up their . . . you know . . .
An iron bar . . . Or maybe a sharpened elk's horn.

V

The Forum Shops in Caesar's Palace. A CHORUS *of Romans is milling around.* TACO *and* DUMDUM *make their way over to the fountain of Poseidon, who carries a trident in one hand, a dolphin in the other.*

DUMDUM I think we're on what they call 'the horns
of a dilemma'.

TACO   There's the dolphin,
at any rate.

DUMDUM   That's just great. That's all we need.

TACO   Remember Bono
and the Edge in Las Vegas?

DUMDUM   This place would suit
them fuckers down to the ground.

> TACO *plays air guitar and hums 'I Still Haven't Found What I'm Looking For'.*

DUMDUM   Pretentious
gits . . . Taco.

TACO   Yeah.

DUMDUM   That night in the bar.

TACO What bar?

DUMDUM   McSorleys.

TACO   That's ten years ago.

DUMDUM   The
swoop. The strip-
search. The night they shot the Chief.

TACO   The night
they *missed*
Clery.

DUMDUM   It was a cover, wasn't it?

TACO   Ask me no
questions and I'll tell
you no lies. What makes you think of it?

DUMDUM   Those
two very

                        sweaty boys in the airport . . .
TACO
                                            Trench and Trilby
                        . . . That's their uniform.
DUMDUM   Trilby . . . Made me think of Gilbey.
TACO
                                                    I suppose
                    that, in its way,
                    The Joshua Tree is an attack on the soft centre
                    of contemporary America.
DUMDUM
                                            A soft target.
TACO
                                                    I still
                    prefer it to *Zooropa*. Songs like 'Lemon',
                    or 'Babyface'. They're total crap.
DUMDUM
                                            All that crap
                    about the Red Hand
                    Commandos shooting Gilbey. A cover.
TACO
                                            That's just
                    change
                    for the sake of change. 'Less is more,'
                    as Bono says. Or maybe it's 'More is less.'
                    'Babyface'. It's about a centre-fold.
DUMDUM   Not 'Babyface' Nelson?
TACO   No.
DUMDUM   Not 'Bugsy' Siegel?
                    Not 'Legs'
                    Diamond?

                    TACO *calls out through the crowd.*

TACO   Engelbert.
DUMDUM   Engelbert?
TACO   Humperdinck.
DUMDUM   You're kidding.
TACO   No. That was him. Either that or
                    'a loose
                    interpretation of the original'. Like 'The Fly'.
DUMDUM   'The Fly'?
TACO   This character Bono invented. Part
                    Elvis.
                    Part Engelbert. My da loved them.

                                                            21

DUMDUM   Who? U2?

TACO   Engelbert. Tom Jones. He'd pour a bottle of
                Red Heart
            and light up a Gallaher's Blue.
            Red Heart. With a wee Bell's whiskey on the
                side. Bell's for a Bell.
            The Billy Cotton Bandshow. Every week they'd
                book
            either Tom Jones or Engelbert Humperdinck.
            Now they're playing at the Sands.

DUMDUM   The only Sands that matters, Taco, is Bobby Sands.
            A hunger-striker choking on his own Adam's-
                apple.

TACO   Those were the days, Dumdum.

DUMDUM   After sixty-six
            days, Taco.

TACO   Those were the days.

VI

TACO and DUMDUM wander off around the Forum Shops. Unbeknownst to them, DOLL enters, dressed to kill in a flared pants suit of a blue not found in nature. She carries the bulky manila envelope.

DOLL   The thing I love about Vegas is that the days
and nights are the same. The sky is always blue.
Like a computer screen. Like a Mac Apple.
A submarine world glimpsed from a diving-bell.
Liquid crystal. Silicon chips. A world built of
    sand.
The laptop world. The world of the Powerbook.
A world of power and plenty. Shrimp cocktail,
    chowder, clam strips.
They overflow from Triton's horn.
Pearls before swine in the oyster-bar.
The pearls are phoney. The oysters are phoney.
The swine wear bibs over their leisure-suits.
My mother didn't know
if my father was some hot-shit senator
or the slob who played Subtle. She was in *The
    Alchemist*
at the time. She got herself in the family way
half-way through a twenty city tour. When she
    filled out hotel
registration forms
she always gave her name as 'The Queen of
    Fairy'.
But only gradually did it unfold
that she named me 'Doll' after 'Dol Common'
though, of course, she spelt it with two 'l's
rather than one.

    *TACO and DUMDUM begin to move towards DOLL.
    She moves accordingly, so as not to be seen.
    DUMDUM points to his watch.*

DUMDUM   Look, Taco. The little hand
            is at six . . .
      DOLL   Not that she can spell any more.
            She's suffered such a sea-change
            since the last time they patched up her heart
            with a vein out of her leg.
            That really cut me up . . .
DUMDUM   The big hand's
            drawing level.
      DOLL Six-thirty. The thing I love about Vegas is that
               you have to think
            about whether it's a.m. or p.m. Now she lives in
               a retirement home in Tenafly.
            She's not herself though. There's a screw loose.

VII

As DOLL *turns away,* VERA *enters and makes her way towards* TACO *and* DUMDUM. *A strikingly beautiful, if somewhat androgynous, black woman,* VERA *flaunts a copy of* The Economist. TACO *and* DUMDUM *are somewhat taken aback.*

VERA   Mr Bell?

TACO   Could be.

VERA   Vera Loman.

DUMDUM   Say nothing,
Taco. Loose
lips sink ships.

TACO   My heart
just skipped a beat.

VERA   Come quickly. We must fly.

TACO   Fly? Fly where?

VERA   I'll explain everything.

TACO   I wouldn't
mind throwing the leg
over this one. What do you think?

VERA   'Two vast and
trunkless legs . . . The lone and level . . . '

DUMDUM   Think? *Always* judge a book
by its cover. That's what I think.

TACO *is quite evidently taken with* VERA.

TACO   'Ozymandias'?

VERA   'Boundless and bare the lone and level sands
stretch far away.'

DUMDUM   It's all over now, Baby Blue.

VERA   It's only beginning, Mr Bell.

TACO   Call me Taco.

VERA   Call me Vera. Now, let's go over to
Hippolyta.

DUMDUM   Sure. Sure. Let's hobble
over to Hippolyfuckingta.

VERA *ushers* TACO *and* DUMDUM *away.*

VERA   It's a new casino
that's opened just off the Strip.

As VERA, DUMDUM *and* TACO *exit,* DOLL *clutches the manila envelope to her breast.*

DOLL I used to think that everything I did was in pursuit
of the truth. That I was a Gate of Horn
through which the shades of truth would pass. My
    job is to put Taco Bell and Dumdum Devlin
behind bars.
But the Gate of Horn and the Gate of Ivory
have been torn down. Torn asunder.

TRENCH and TRILBY enter and lurk in the background in their usual obvious way.

I can't tell what's what. All I see are spirit-forms
through a scrim of mist.
There's no way to tell. No way to tell
the false dreams from the true. No way.
The time has come for me to make a change.
I've had enough of men who fold
newspapers under their arms. There'll be no more
loading the dice. I've had enough of being a
    lemon.
Enough of being a snitch. Enough of the under-
    hand.
The thing I love about Vegas is the hoping more,
    not the having less.

VIII

DOLL *exits, followed by* TRENCH *and* TRILBY. *The scene shifts to the hustle-bustle of the blackjack and roulette tables, video poker and slot machines in Hippolyta, where a* CHORUS *of casino girls are wheeling and dealing.*

CASINO GIRLS   And so, by hoping more, they have but less.
Those that most covet must scatter and unloose
    their change
to a slot machine. Theirs is always a losing hand.
There's no knowing when to hold and when to
    fold.
No knowing how the oranges and lemons
might line up. And so they have but less by
    hoping more.

    VERA *enters, leading* TACO *and* DUMDUM *through the casino to a bank of slot machines.*

The king and the commoner. All are made level.
For what they have not, that which they possess
    they scatter and unloose
from their bond.

    VERA *takes a casino girl by the arm and points to a machine.*

VERA   Tight or loose?

    The girl nods. VERA *starts to play the machine.*

TACO   Hey, Dumdum. What do you think?
DUMDUM   I think 'Portrush'. I think 'Bundoran'. I think of
    the heart
of darkness. Of a fly rubbing its legs.
TACO   Get over yourself.
DUMDUM   I think of a big, fat fly

sitting on a pile of shit and playing the double bass.

VERA *continues to play the slot machine.* TACO *and* DUMDUM *look on.*

CASINO GIRLS   Oranges and lemons and pineapples.
No knowing how they might line up. They come armed with books
on how to beat the system. Oranges and lemons. The bells
of St Clements.

TACO   You see *School Daze*?

DUMDUM   Nope.

TACO   She reminds me of an actress in *School Daze*.

DUMDUM   Black and fucking blue.
They beat Gilbey black and blue. Death by a thousand
cuts. You see *The Crying Game*, Taco? That'll knock your socks off. Hit him over the head with an iron fucking bar.

There's an explosive payoff from VERA'S *slot machine.*

VERA   Bar . . . Bar . . . Bar . . .

CASINO GIRLS   There's no knowing how they might line up . . . No . . .
And yet these patsies in their Teflon
jackets and ski-pants fastened by Velcro strips —
these stooges, these suckers, these tinhorns —
they've the nerve to think they might have a winning suit,
the nerve to think they might have found a way to beat the system.

VERA *has gathered her winnings into her purse and is making her way back to* TACO *and* DUMDUM.

Only the likes of Vera
can truly show and tell
what lies at the epicentre
of Las Vegas while those that most covet
imagine they must
be caught up in schemes and scams and
strategies and the so-called 'study of form'.

IX

DOLL *enters, still carrying the manila envelope, and intercepts* VERA.

DOLL Vera.

VERA   Doll.

DOLL   How are you? How's the form?

VERA Just as good as it can be, girl. You know the way
it is.

DOLL   I do believe I do.

As they embrace, DOLL *registers* VERA's *fragrance.*

Love in the Mist?

VERA *Persistence*, child. *Persistence.* Got it through an in-
flight magazine . . . Jojoba . . . Aloe vera . . .
All that good stuff. Otherwise I'd be burned to a
cinder.

DOLL Elizabeth Taylor?

VERA   Elizabeth, New Jersey . . . Do tell
me more about our Irish friends.

DOLL   More?

VERA Why are you on their case?

DOLL *glimpses* TRENCH *and* TRILBY *looming larger
than ever.*

They seem so . . .
harmless.

DOLL I'll be with you in the squeezing of a lemon,
as my mother used to say.

DOLL *clasps the manila envelope and goes in the
direction of* TRENCH *and* TRILBY.

I'm just going to ex-
change
a dress in Saks.

VERA, *too, has become aware of* TRENCH *and* TRILBY. *She holds* DOLL *back.*

VERA   You're being followed,
aren't you?

DOLL   Oh, Vera . . .

VERA   I don't like the way
they keep their hands
inside their lapels.

DOLL   Oh, Vera . . . Extreme fear can
neither fight nor fly.
They look like fools. But I once saw Trench level
a Magnum at some poor Mexican kid and shoot
 off half his leg.
Talk about being footloose
and fancy free. And Trilby . . . Trilby would stick
 a knife through your heart
without batting an eyelid.

VERA   Do you think
we should bat *our* eyelids at *them*?

DOLL   Too late. The
 sands
of time, Vera, were already running out when I
 called you from somewhere over Minneapolis.
It wasn't just a whim. It wasn't a bolt from the
 blue.

VERA No?

DOLL Oh, Vera . . . It's the oldest trick in the book.

VERA How so?

DOLL   Somebody from the DA's
office wanted to set you up along with Taco Bell
and Dumdum Devlin. Something about a
 lawsuit?

VERA I knew it. I knew it. It has to do with a little
 sidebar
I had with a judge. A lot of side. A lot of bar.
I charged him with aggravated assault. They've
 been trying to get me to draw in my horns
for two years. To drop the suit. I've been saying no.

VERA *draws* DOLL *to her.*

It's alright, child. We'll lose Trench and Trilby on
the Strip.
Come on, my men. Let's see what gives at
Delphine.

X

TRENCH *and* TRILBY *look on dumbfoundedly as* DOLL *pointedly abandons the manila envelope.* VERA *ushers* DOLL, TACO *and* DUMDUM *out of the casino. The scene shifts to Delphine, a strip club pulsating to the bump and grind of a chorus of strippers and lapdancers.*

DANCERS We come into the world as we go out of
Delphine —
in the buff, in our birthday suits.
STRIPPERS So it follows that we strip
till we break our balls and our birth's invidious
bar.
DANCERS *With a hey and a ho and a hey nonny no*
STRIPPERS Till we grasp the skirts of happy chance
and the bull by its brass-tipped horns.
DANCERS For we're earthy girls, though it's hard to tell
from just looking at our heavenly forms.
STRIPPERS *With a hey and a ho and a hey nonny no*

VERA *enters with* DOLL, TACO *and* DUMDUM. *They make their way to a table near the runway.*

DANCERS For this is it. This is the centre
of Vegas. The centre of America. When it seems
there's no way
out of the maze . . .
STRIPPERS When you stumble as in a
reverie
through a cold and heavy mist . . .

DUMDUM *is clearly agitated.*

DUMDUM Gilbey was only a week out of Long Kesh. We
tied his hands
with a bit of flex.
TACO Shut the fuck up.

33

DUMDUM   Took him to a
             bog not far from Carrickmore.
             He was stumbling around. Wearing a blindfold.
             I can still hear the wheeping of curlews.

             TACO *gets up, takes* VERA's *hand.*

    TACO Come with me, Vera, I seriously need a change
             of address.

             TACO *and* VERA *exit, leaving* DUMDUM *and* DOLL.

DANCERS   When all seems lost, sweet pal o'
             mine,
             you'll find yourself in Delphine.
STRIPPERS   And please
             don't think
             we're into Dutch caps . . .
DANCERS   French ticklers . . .
STRIPPERS   Or
             Spanish fly . . .
DANCERS Please don't think that we wear our hearts
             on our sleeves.
STRIPPERS   We don't even wear sleeves.
DANCERS   And
             just because you're eye-level
             with our butts doesn't mean we're Appaloosas.
             Doesn't mean we're ready to ride.
STRIPPERS   Just because
             we show a bit of leg
             doesn't mean we're the Belles
             of Hell.
DANCERS   Just because you want to see blood on
             the sand
             at the Circus Maximus.
STRIPPERS   Just because you want to
             seize the day
             doesn't mean you can grasp the Appaloosa's
             mane or flowing tail as you might grasp the

34

skirts of happy chance
DANCERS *With a hey and a ho and a hey nonny no*

DUMDUM *is still clearly agitated.*

DUMDUM Taggart said it was alright. It was done according to the Green Book.

DUMDUM *turns to* DOLL.

Where's Taco?
STRIPPERS *With a hey and a ho and a hey nonny no*
DOLL   With Vera.
I believe he's making her brown eyes blue.
DANCERS ⎱ For we above all have grasped the skirts of
AND ⎰   happy chance
STRIPPERS ⎰ and breasted the blows of circumstance.
With a hey and a ho and a hey nonny no.

XI

As the CHORUS *exit,* TACO *hurries in, clearly discombobulated, and makes his way towards* DUMDUM *and* DOLL.

TACO   Dumdum. Dumdum. Dumdum.

DUMDUM   You can talk
till you're blue
in the face.

TACO   Dumdum.

DUMDUM   I'll just ignore you.

TACO   Dumdum. It
seems that little Miss Lulabelle
isn't everything she seems.

DUMDUM   With a hey . . .

TACO   It's
like something out of a dirty book.

DUMDUM   And a ho . . .

TACO   I gave her a peck on the cheek. Her
chin's like sand-
paper.

DUMDUM   And a hey . . .

TACO   She has an Adam's-apple.

DUMDUM   Nonny . . .

TACO   And, Dumdum, when I had a feel of
little Lady Day
she had this huge fucking horn.

DUMDUM   No.

TACO   Like the horn on a fucking gramophone.

DUMDUM   No?

TACO His Master's Voice, Dumdum.

DUMDUM   She always
struck me as a shade . . . hirsute . . .

TACO *Hir*sute? *His*fuckingsute.

DUMDUM   What happened next?

TACO   It was like a crowbar,
Dumdum.

DUMDUM   What happened next?

TACO   I wanted to
tear a strip
off her . . . off him . . . for leading me on . . .

DUMDUM   You
mightn't have missed
it if you'd seen *The Crying Game*. Didn't I tell
you?

TACO   Then a strange thing happened.

DUMDUM   You're not
doing a McAnespie? You're not turning into a
fairy?

TACO   A strange thing happened. It just came to me.
That these are just different forms
of one thing. That there's no right way.
There's no right. No left. There's no centre.

DUMDUM   No, Taco.

TACO   I knew that I felt somehow . . . close
. . . to Vera Loman.

DUMDUM   Low-man by name and Low-man by nature. So
. . . Let me get this straight. You're standing
there with your hand
up this guy's skirt and you decide it's all change
at Piccafuckingdilly.

TACO   It struck me that men and
women are more
or less the same.

DUMDUM   Would you say 'more' or 'less'?

TACO   What's the difference? A bit of loose skin . . . a fold
of flesh . . .

DUMDUM   And what about Vera's middle leg?
Have you had a chance to think
about that?

TACO   Dumdum.

DUMDUM   It sounds as if we're
talking about more than a bit of loose . . .

TACO   Dumdum.

DUMDUM   Skin.

TACO   Then he started to unbutton the
fly . . .

DUMDUM No, Taco.

TACO   Of my Levis . . .

DUMDUM No, Taco.

TACO   I didn't stop him, Dumdum. I just
            didn't have the heart.

XII

DOLL *makes her way over towards* TACO *and* DUMDUM.

DOLL I just didn't have the heart
to tell you, Taco, that Vera works at the Bootleg.

TACO *fishes in his breast pocket.*

TACO I know.

DUMDUM The Bootleg?

TACO *hands* VERA's *card to* DUMDUM *who studies
it.*

TACO   She's the only one who's
had the guts to level
with me.

DUMDUM   L-A-P-D-A-N-C-E-R-S?

TACO   Don't you think
it's time you came clean, Doll?

VERA *enters and comes towards* TACO, DUMDUM
and DOLL.

DUMDUM   Shoo, fly. Shoo, fly.

TACO Put a sock in it.

DOLL   It's simple, Taco. Two illegal
aliens are on the loose
in Las Vegas.

VERA   I can just see the headline in *New
York Newsday:*
'Wacko Taco Backo'.

DOLL   'Federal agents in Las Vegas
blew
away two Irish Republican Army worms who
tried to wriggle out of the Big Apple.
Dumdum Devlin and Taco Bell . . . '

DUMDUM Devine.

VERA   Thank you, darling.

DOLL   The blood on the
sand
will be yours, Dumdum. Trench and Trilby don't
do things by the book.
They're Brits, you see. Ex-MI5. They were stripped
of their ranks after an incident on the Matterhorn.
Had to do with a hausfrau and an ice-pick.

TACO   Wunderbar.

DUMDUM It's Devine. Not Devlin.

DOLL   Devlin. Devine. You think it'll matter diddly-
squat to that pair in the pinstripe suits?
You don't mess with those guys. It's an absolute
no-no.

VERA   I've an idea.

DUMDUM   Hey ho.

VERA   Why don't Alexander
and I get married?

DOLL   Alexander? I must have
missed
something here.

DUMDUM   Alexander Graham Bell.

TACO   That
way
the INS will back off.

DOLL   Of course.

VERA   Precisely.

DUMDUM Trench? Trilby?

VERA   I could tell
you stuff about Trench and Trilby that would
make your hair curl.

DUMDUM   Whips?

DOLL   Chains?

DUMDUM   School-
girls' uniforms?

DOLL   You know, Dumdum, I could become very, very,
very
fond of you.

DUMDUM   Hey ho.
VERA   May I borrow my card?

VERA *recovers her card from* DUMDUM. *She folds and tears it.*

                                            If I
fold
it like so . . . and tear it like so . . .

VERA *hands it to* DOLL.

DOLL   I didn't know
your real name was Allemagne . . .
VERA It's not . . .

DOLL *returns the card to* VERA *who puts it in her purse.* TACO *sidles up to* VERA.

TACO   Vera, Vera, Vera of Las
Vegas . . .
VERA   Perhaps you'll do me the honour of
taking my hand?
TACO I most definitely will.
VERA   It shouldn't take more
than ten minutes.
DUMDUM   I can't take much more
of this.
TACO   How much will it cost?

VERA *raises her purse with her casino winnings.*

VERA   There's still
plenty left in the bureau de change.
DUMDUM Next thing you know he'll be having a sex-
change.

XIII

All exit. The scene shifts to a wedding chapel complete with a pre-recorded CHOIR.

CHOIR   The ever-whirling wheel of change
     brings us back to God as sheep unto the fold,
     brings us back to the subliminal text of *Amor*
     Vincit Omnia. As we know, the word subliminal
      comes from *limen,*
     'a threshold' and *sub,* 'under'. Many who have
      had first hand
     experience of both the bitter aloes
     of life and the love of God will deem themselves
      unworthy to unloose
     the latchet of His shoes. Yet a broken and a
      contrite heart,
     O God, thou wilt not despise.

     DUMDUM *and* TACO *enter.*

              For man is born
     into trouble, as the sparks fly
     upward, as grave Alice, and laughing Allegra,
     and Edith with the golden hair fly upward, as
      the divine thought thinks
     of itself, though at a subliminal level.
TACO   Thinking a divine thought, Dumdum?

     DUMDUM *sulks.*

CHOIR   For as
     the Good Book
     reminds us, who can number the days
     of eternity, and the drops of rain, and the sand
     of the sea?

     As VERA *enters with* DOLL, TACO *and* DUMDUM

hide behind a Doric column.

DOLL   Something old.
VERA   Something new.
               Something borrowed.
VERA   Something blue.
DOLL Do you, Alexander Graham Taco Bell,
      take this woman to be your lawful wife?
CHOIR   For long
         before Eve gave Adam the apple
         and Noah . . .
VERA   What if he says no?
CHOIR   Before Noah
      begat Shem, Ham and Japheth and, eyeless in
         the Gaza Strip,
      Samson ignored Delilah's suit,
      long, long before Joshua blew his horn,
      long before the flood itself, long ante the
         antedeluvian . . .
DOLL If anyone knows of any impediment, any bar
      to this marriage . . .

          DUMDUM *throws up his hands.*

VERA   Let him speak now or
         forever hold his peashooter.
DOLL   For very, very,
      verily I say unto ye, what God has joined let no
      man put asunder.

          VERA *picks up a couple of forms from a stack by the
          altar.*

VERA Here, Doll, why don't you take one of these forms
      and fill it out?
DOLL   For myself and Dumdum?

          DUMDUM *winces at the thought.*

CHOIR   Behold,
              I show you a myst-
         ery, as Paul wrote in his First Epistle
         to the Corinthians; We shall not sleep, we shall
            all be bound on the ever-whirling wheel of
                change, the which all mortal things doth sway.

XIV

DOLL busies herself with a form while VERA takes centre stage.

VERA For I, Vera of Las Vegas, am the Way,
    the Truth and the Light. I who seem to be on the
      periphery
    of things am, truth to tell,
    at the very centre.
    I who seem shrouded in mist
    am as clear as daylight. For it's only through
      their outward forms
    that things truly show themselves. The more we
      change the less
    we truly change.
    For truth's a business that needs a little illusion,
      a little sleight-of-hand,
    if it's not to fold,
    if it's not to go belly-up.

> *TRENCH and TRILBY enter, TRENCH clutching the
> manila envelope, and lurk behind a Doric column
> opposite TACO and DUMDUM.*

               The night I met His
    Honour at the Palomino
    we went belly-up, alright. The more I gave him
      the more
    he wanted. He tasted of falafel.
    Falafel or hummus. His falafellatious Honour.
      Now does he feel his title hang loose
    about him. Is there a man of woman born who
      doesn't think
    the way to a girl's heart
    is a slap in the face?

> *TRENCH and TRILBY move into VERA's line of
> vision.*

I'm at my wit's end now.
I'm on my last legs.
And I still don't know, with the great Chuang
Tzu, if I'm a man dreaming I'm a butterfly
or a butterfly dreaming I'm a man.

She breaks off, as if arriving at something.

What I already knew at the age of ten, when I
found myself hankering after a sailor-suit
in a store-window, one of those blue and white
suits worn by Tadzio
in *Death in Venice*, was that I'd have to find a way
to scrape the red clay
off my boots. My father asked me to wait till the
sow had had her farrow.
Would that I might tread them in my anger, and
trample them in my fury,
those who trod and trampled him. Poor man.
Poor ne're-do-well.
Had he been William Tell
aiming at an apple on his son's head while an
Austrian sentry
trained a crossbow on him, he'd have missed by
a century.
Poor ne'er-do-well . . . He'd have missed.
Next thing I knew the sow had died from eating
too much beech-mast
and he had to sell the farm.
No sailor-suit. No nothing. By this time I'd
taken to imagining my form
in a little strapless, backless
number worn by the lady on the cover of
Gentlemen Prefer Blondes by Anita Loos.
This was 1963. By this time my mind was
opening to the endless range
of possibilities, to the great change
come sweeping through America, come sweeping across the land,

whereby the great-great-grandson of slaves and
    the son of a field-hand
could struggle out of the pig-pen or the sheep-
    fold
in which his great-great-grandfathers had been
    bought and sold
and stand tall. I was wrong . . . I think of those
    who've trodden and trampled Vera Loman
and called her 'love' and 'lady' and 'such a leman'
while thinking of her as just another whore
and my anger deepens as, more and more,
I realise I've swapped one hovel
for another. And I've come to see that, while on
    one level
I have such power as beauty brings, on another
    I'm quite powerless.
I hate that. I hate these blowhard Abelards who
    see me as Heloïse,
these ashen Aschenbachs coughing into their drinks
who have the nerve to think
that underneath it all, in my heart of hearts,
I'm some skinny-assed Tadzio. I'm not Tadzio.
    I'm not that little simpering fart.
And yet . . . And yet . . . And yet I'm tied down
    by an iron peg
just as my great-grandfather, Virgil, was chained
    by his left leg
to a mounting-block. And yet . . . And yet . . . He
    saw the Lord sitting upon a throne and above
        it stood the seraphims and each one had six
            wings; with twain he covered his face and
                with twain he covered his feet, and with
                    twain he did fly.

TRENCH *and* TRILBY *begin to move towards* VERA,
who notices them for the first time.

Then there's the storekeeper in Tennessee who
    shot my uncle for stealing a pineapple

and was never brought to book.
That set off an alarm-bell
in my grandmother's head. Rather than sit out
    her days
eating watermelon and singing the blues
she decided to do something about it. She drew
    a line in the sand.
Sometimes you have to take a stand just as she
    took a stand against the colour-bar.

VERA *moves purposefully towards* TRENCH *and*
TRILBY, *searching in her purse and recovering the*
card, which she presents to TRENCH.

If I may trouble you, Signorina Capote.

TRENCH *briefly examines the card, fidgets, and*
passes it to TRILBY, *whom* VERA *now addresses.*

                                    Signorina
    Barsolino.

TRILBY *also fidgets and begins to move away as*
VERA *again rummages in her purse.*

I have here warrants for the arrests of Signorina
    Norma Capote and Signorina Lucia Barsolino
        for the murder, by ice-pick tipped with the
            alkaloid *Delphinine*,
of a Fraülein Maria Von Trapp, formerly of
    Gundestrup,
whose body was discovered last week on the
    slopes of the Matterhorn.

TRENCH *and* TRILBY *exchange horrified glances.*

She was identified only by dental records and
    her ski-suit.

XV

TRENCH *drops the manila envelope,* TRILBY *the card. They exit hurriedly, casting off their outer garments and revealing themselves to be women.*

TRENCH⎫
TRILBY⎭ Zut! Zut! Zut! Zut! Zut!

> TACO, DUMDUM *and* DOLL *emerge from the shadows.* TACO *picks up the card and studies it.*

TACO Vera Allemagne . . . (*Spelling it out*) L-A-P-D . . .

TRENCH⎫
TRILBY⎭ Zut! Zut! Zut! Zut! Zut!

DOLL That's what I call 'Exit, pursued
by a bear.'

> TACO *sings to the tune of 'Davy Crockett'.*

TACO 'Born on a mountaintop in Tennessee.
Killed her a bar
when she was only three.'

DUMDUM Swanlinbar.

TACO You what?

DUMDUM That's where they found Dessie
Gillespie slumped over the horn
of a Ford Escort. That's what matters. Not this
shit about the Matterhorn.
It makes no sense.

TACO He who knows does not speak,
Dumdum. He who speaks does not know.

DOLL Nothing is what it seems. Even 'Nevada' means
'covered with snow'.
That's why we have to strip
everything down like the transmission on a Ford.

DUMDUM Is that why you put a strip
of duct-tape over his mouth? On the road

between Killyhevlin and Swanlinbar. Remember? You pumped him full of lead.

TACO *corrects* DUMDUM.

TACO   *Glangevlin.*
DUMDUM Glangevlin.
TACO   It has to do with being able to trans-
form
lead into gold, Dumdum.
DOLL   You must transfigure
and transform
yourself, Dumdum. You must find a way
not to stand in your own way.
You must become an alchemist.
DUMDUM Mist is the word, Taco. We're in a bog. We're lost
in a mist.
It makes no sense. We know nothing about Doll.
We know nothing about Vera.
TACO That's true of everyone. That's true of every
aspect of our lives.
DOLL   Have you sometimes seen a
cloud that looks like a centaur?
VERA A camel?
DOLL   A weasel?
VERA   A whale?
DUMDUM   I saw a bomb go
off in the centre
of Belfast. At the Europa Hotel.
It had a cloud, so far as I could tell,
that looked like a cloud.
DOLL   I like you more and more,
Dumdum. More and more. And then some more.
To most people, nothing looks less
like a cloud than a cloud. You see things for what
they are.
DUMDUM   What about that Los
Angeles Police Department shit? What happens
when Trench and Trilby find out they've been

sold a lemon
by this Vera Allemagne?
What happens when they find out they've been
given short change?

VERA We won't see them again. Don't worry.

DOLL   I've
changed, Dumdum. You can change
too, if you like.

VERA   The thought of a couple of
thousand volts
up the ass should keep those she-wolves away
from the fold.

DOLL Come, Dumdum. Give me your hand.

DUMDUM *takes* DOLL's *hand.*

DUMDUM I've seen a cloud . . .

DOLL   Yes?

DUMDUM   No bigger . . .

DOLL   Yes?

DUMDUM   Than
a man's hand.

DOLL Yes, Dumdum?

DUMDUM *embraces* DOLL. *Swept up by the flood of
emotion,* TACO *embraces* VERA. DUMDUM *is now
transported.*

DUMDUM I once saw a bomb go off in Belfast.
It had a cloud that, so far as I could tell,
looked exactly like a cloud.
Just like a cloud.

TACO *seems spent.* DOLL *holds him reassuringly.*
TACO *now holds* VERA *at arm's length.*

TACO I'd give anything to be a fly
on the wall when Trench and Trilby realize what
a fly

boy you are. Their car will have stalled on a level-
crossing and the Chattanooga Choochoo will be
drawing level
with them and it'll hit them you've pulled their
legs.

VERA That's why we must go through with the wedding.

DUMDUM *and* DOLL *move closer to* VERA.

TACO Wedding?
I can't go through with a wedding.

TACO *steps back from* VERA. *He sinks into a chair
as if unconscious. His hands are cuffed. The judder
of blood in his ears. The lights fade as the bright
lamp descends.* TACO *seems to regain consciousness
and makes what sounds like a confession.*

I shot
Gillespie in both legs.
I still hear the wheep of curlews,
the buzz of bluebottles or clegs
and then a minute's silence, more or less,
before I shot him through his dicky heart.
But, no matter what Dumdum thinks,
I took absolutely no part
in topping Gilbey.

DUMDUM *picks up the manila envelope, weighs it,
puts it to his ear.*

DUMDUM That's funny. I thought I heard it ticking. Why
do you think
Trench and Trilby kept passing the parcel?

DOLL Those
finks
have seen too many James Bond flicks.

DUMDUM I should
probably be doing this behind a bag of sand.

0258

TACO   Dumdum . . . A soft-nosed bullet that expands
on impact . . . I stood outside the chapel
where Gilbey lay, stuffed with sawdust or sand,
in a closed coffin. Someone had blown his
   Adam's-apple
clean away . . . Dumdum . . . That's who . . .

DUMDUM *again puts the manila envelope to his ear.*

DUMDUM   It *is* ticking.

VERA   Mon dieu!

DOLL   Sacre bleu!

DUMDUM *drops the envelope at* TACO's *feet.* DUM-
DUM *and* DOLL *lope off, hand in hand.* VERA *looks
to* TACO, *who turns away from her.* VERA *exits.*

TACO   Gilbey's head looked like a ham on a hook . . .
Someone had knocked him into a bag of blue . . .
Dumdum claims that someone took a leaf from
   his book
to make people think he blew Gilbey away . . .
Ward, maybe . . . Or Clery . . . Someone else in
   the cell . . .
We may have to wait until Judgement Day
before all is revealed . . .

VERA   (*Off*)   Taco . . .

TACO *looks about.*

VERA   (*A wail*) Where's
my Taco Bell?

*The judder of the blood and the shudder of a plane
taking off. Fade to black.*